OUR AMERICA!

I pledge allegiance
to the flag
of the United States of America
and to the republic
for which it stands,
one nation,
under God,
indivisible,
with liberty
and justice for all.

ideals

A National Prayer

Thomas Jefferson

Almighty God, who has given us this good land
For our heritage, we humbly beseech Thee
That we may always prove ourselves a people mindful
Of Thy favor and glad to do Thy will.

Bless our land with honorable industry,
Sound learning, and pure manners.
Save us from violence, discord, and confusion;
From pride and arrogance, and from every evil way.
Defend our liberties, and fashion into one united people
The multitude brought hither out of many kindreds and tongues.

Endow with the spirit of wisdom those to whom in Thy Name
We entrust the authority of government,
That there may be justice and peace at home,
And that through obedience to Thy law,
We may show forth Thy praise
Among the nations of the earth.

In time of prosperity,
Fill our hearts with thankfulness,
And, in the day of trouble, suffer not
Our trust in Thee to fail;
All of which we ask
Through Jesus Christ our Lord,
Amen.

Painting Opposite
AMERICAN FLAG AND EAGLE
George Hinke

GIVE ME LIBERTY OR GIVE ME DEATH

There is a just God who presides over the destinies of nations and who will raise up friends to fight our battles for us. The battle, sir, is not to the strong alone; it is to the vigilant, the active, the brave. Besides, sir, we have no election. If we were base enough to desire it, it is now too late to retire from the contest. There is no retreat but in submission and slavery! Our chains are forged! Their clanking may be heard on the plains of Boston! The war is inevitable—and let it come! I repeat, sir, let it come!

It is in vain, sir, to extenuate the matter. Gentlemen may cry, Peace, Peace—but there is no peace. The war is actually begun! The next gale that sweeps from the north will bring to our ears the clash of resounding arms! Our brethren are already in the field! Why stand we here idle? What is it that gentlemen wish? What would they have? Is life so dear, or peace so sweet, as to be purchased at the price of chains and slavery? Forbid it, Almighty God! I know not what course the others may take; but as for me, give me liberty or give me death!

Patrick Henry

CONCORD HYMN

Ralph Waldo Emerson

By the rude bridge that arched the flood,
    Their flag to April's breeze unfurled,
Here once the embattled farmers stood
    And fired the shot heard round the world.

The foe long since in silence slept;
    Alike the conqueror silent sleeps;
And time the ruined bridge has swept
    Down the dark stream which seaward creeps.

On this green bank, by this soft stream,
    We set today a votive stone;
That memory may their deeds redeem,
    When, like our sires, our sons are gone.

Spirit, that made those heroes dare
    To die and leave their children free,
Bid Time and Nature gently spare
    The shaft we raise to them and thee.

Photo Opposite
THE MINUTEMAN
Lexington, Massachusetts
FPG International

THE DECLARATION OF INDEPENDENCE

When, in the course of human events, it becomes necessary for one people to dissolve the political bands which have connected them with another, and to assume, among the Powers of the earth, the separate and equal station to which the Laws of Nature and of Nature's God entitle them, a decent respect to the opinions of mankind requires that they should declare the causes which impel them to the separation.

We hold these truths to be self-evident: that all men are created equal; that they are endowed by their Creator with certain inalienable Rights; that among these are Life, Liberty, and the Pursuit of Happiness. That, to secure these Rights, Governments are instituted among Men, deriving their just powers from the consent of the governed. That, whenever any Form of Government becomes destructive of these ends, it is the Right of the People to alter or to abolish it, and to institute new Government, laying its foundation on such Principles, and organizing its Powers in such form, as to them shall seem most likely to effect their Safety and Happiness.

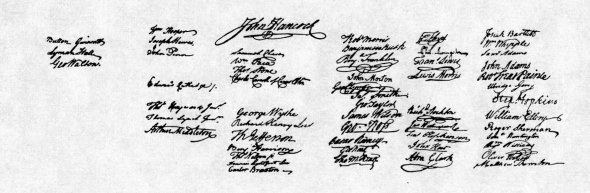

A NATION'S STRENGTH

Ralph Waldo Emerson

What makes a nation's pillars high
And its foundations strong?
What makes it mighty to defy
The foes that round it throng?

It is not gold. Its kingdoms grand
Go down in battle shock;
Its shafts are laid on sinking sand,
Not on abiding rock.

Is it the sword? Ask the red dust
Of empires passed away;
The blood has turned their stones to rust,
Their glory to decay.

And is it pride? Ah, that bright crown
Has seemed to nations sweet;
But God has struck its luster down
In ashes at his feet.

Not gold but only men can make
A people great and strong;
Men who for truth and honor's sake
Stand fast and suffer long.

Brave men who work while others sleep,
Who dare while others fly—
They build a nation's pillars deep
And lift them to the sky.

THE BIRTH OF A NATION

Yesterday, the greatest question was decided, which ever was debated in America, and a greater, perhaps, never was nor will be decided among men. A resolution was passed without one dissenting colony, "that these United Colonies are, and of rights ought to be, free and independent States, and as such they have, and of right ought to have, full power to make war, conclude peace, establish commerce, and to do all other acts and things which other States may rightfully do." You will see in a few days a declaration setting forth the causes which have impelled us to this mighty revolution, and the reasons which will justify it in the sight of God and man. A plan of confederation will be taken up in a few days.

You will think me transported with enthusiasm, but I am not. I am well aware of the toil, and blood, and treasure, that it will cost us to maintain this declaration, and support and defend these States. Yet, through all the gloom, I can see the rays of ravishing light and glory. I can see that the end is more than worth all the means, and that posterity will triumph in that day's transaction, even though we should rue it, which I trust in God we shall not.

John Adams

THE AMERICAN CRISIS

These are the times that try men's souls. The summer soldier and the sunshine patriot will, in this crisis, shrink from the service of their country; but he that stands it now deserves the love and thanks of man and woman. Tyranny, like Hell, is not easily conquered; yet we have this consolation with us, that the harder the conflict, the more glorious the triumph. What we obtain too cheap, we esteem too lightly; it is dearness only that gives every thing its value. Heaven knows how to put a proper price upon its goods; and it would be strange indeed if so celestial an article as Freedom should not be highly rated.

Thomas Paine

Photo Opposite
MILITIA FIFE AND DRUM
Colonial Williamsburg Foundation
Williamsburg, Virginia

GOD GIVE US MEN

Josiah Gilbert Holland

God, give us Men! A time like this demands
Strong minds, great hearts, true faith and ready hands;
Men whom the lust of office does not kill;
Men whom the spoils of office cannot buy;
Men who possess opinions and a will;
Men who have honor; men who will not lie;
Men who can stand before a demagogue
And damn his treacherous flatteries without winking!
Tall men, sun-crowned, who live above the fog
In public duty and in private thinking;
For while the rabble, with their thumb-worn creeds,
Their large professions and their little deeds,
Mingle in selfish strife, lo! Freedom weeps,
Wrong rules the land, and waiting Justice sleeps.

Painting Opposite
THE SPIRIT OF '76
A. M. Willard

THE FLAG OF OUR COUNTRY

There is the national flag. He must be cold indeed who can look upon its folds, rippling in the breeze, without pride of country. In a foreign land, the flag is companionship and country itself, with all its endearments.

Who, as he sees it, can think of a state merely? Whose eyes, once fastened upon its radiant trophies, can fail to recognize the image of the whole nation? It has been called a "floating piece of poetry," and yet I know not if it has an intrinsic beauty beyond other ensigns. Its highest beauty is in what it symbolizes. It is because it represents all, that all gaze at it with delight and reverence.

It is a piece of bunting lifted in the air; but it speaks sublimely, and every part has a voice. Its stripes of alternate red and white proclaim the union of thirteen states constituting our national constellation, which receives a new star with every new state. The two together signify union past and present.

The very colors have a language which was officially recognized by our fathers. White is for purity, red for valor, blue for justice; and all together—bunting, stripes, stars, and colors blazing in the sky—make the flag of our country to be cherished by all our hearts, to be upheld by all our hands.

Behold it! Listen to it! Every star has a tongue; every stripe is articulate. There is no speech nor language where their voices are not heard. There is magic in the web of it. It has an answer for every question of duty. It has a word of good cheer for every hour of gloom or of despondency.

Behold it! Listen to it! It speaks of earlier and of later struggles. It speaks of victories and sometimes of reverses, on the sea and on the land. It speaks of patriots and heroes among the living and among the dead; and of him, the first and greatest of them all, around whose consecrated ashes this unnatural and abhorrent strife has so long been raging. But before all and above all other associations and memories, whether of glorious men, or glorious deeds, or glorious places, its voice is ever of union and liberty, of the constitution and of the laws.

Robert C. Winthrop

★★★★★ 18 ★★★★★

Painting Opposite
BETSY ROSS AND THE FLAG
George Hinke

THE BILL OF RIGHTS

1. Congress shall make no law respecting an establishment of religion, or prohibiting the free exercise thereof; or abridging the freedom of speech, or of the press; or the right of the people peaceably to assemble, and to petition the government for a redress of grievances.

2. A well regulated Militia, being necessary to the security of a free State, the right of the people to keep and bear Arms, shall not be infringed.

3. No Soldier shall in time of peace be quartered in any house, without the consent of the Owner, nor in time of war, but in a manner to be prescribed by law.

4. The right of the people to be secure in their persons, houses, papers, and effects, against unreasonable searches and seizures, shall not be violated, and no Warrants shall issue, but upon probable cause, supported by Oath or affirmation, and particularly describing the place to be searched, and the persons or things to be seized.

5. No person shall be held to answer for a capital, or otherwise infamous crime, unless on a presentment or indictment of a Grand Jury, except in cases arising in the land or naval forces, or in the Militia, when in actual service in time of war or public danger; nor shall any person be subject for the same offense to be twice put in jeopardy of life or limb; nor shall be compelled in any criminal case to be a witness against himself, nor be deprived of life, liberty, or property, without due process of law; nor shall private property be taken for public use, without just compensation.

6. In all criminal prosecutions, the accused shall enjoy the right of a speedy and public trial, by an impartial jury of the State and district wherein the crime shall have been committed, which district shall have been previously ascertained by law, and to be informed of the nature and cause of the accusation; to be confronted with the witnesses against him; to have compulsory process for obtaining witnesses in his favor; and to have the Assistance of Counsel for his defense.

7. In Suits at common law, where the value in controversy shall exceed twenty dollars, the right of trial by jury shall be preserved, and no fact tried by jury shall be otherwise re-examined in any Court of the United States, than according to the rules of the common law.

8. Excessive bail shall not be required, nor excessive fines imposed, nor cruel and unusual punishments inflicted.

9. The enumeration in the Constitution of certain rights shall not be construed to deny or disparage others retained by the people.

10. The powers not delegated to the United States by the Constitution, nor prohibited by it to the States, are reserved to the States respectively, or to the people.

First in War— First in Peace

First in war—first in peace—and first in the hearts of his countrymen, he was second to none in the humble and endearing scenes of private life; pious, just, humane, temperate, and sincere; uniform, dignified, and commanding, his example was as edifying to all around him as were the effects of that example lasting.

To his equals, he was condescending, to his inferiors kind, and to the dear objects of his affections exemplarily tender; correct throughout, vice shuddered in his presence, and virtue always felt his fostering hand; the purity of his private character gave effulgence to his public virtues. . . .

Methinks I see his august image, and I hear falling from his venerable lips these deep-sinking words:

"Cease, Sons of America, lamenting our separation; go on, and confirm by your wisdom the fruits of our joint councils, joint efforts, and common dangers; reverence religion, diffuse knowledge throughout your land, patronize the arts and sciences; let Liberty and Order be inseparable companions. Control party spirit, the bane of free governments; observe good faith to, and cultivate peace with all nations, shut up every avenue to foreign influence, contract rather than extend national connection, rely on ourselves only: be Americans in thought, word, and deed;—thus will you give immortality to that union which was the constant object of my terrestrial labors; thus will you preserve undisturbed to the latest posterity the felicity of a people to me most dear, and thus will you supply (if my happiness is now aught to you) the only vacancy in the round of pure bliss high Heaven bestows."

Henry Lee
From an oration in honor of George Washington

Portrait Opposite
GEORGE WASHINGTON
White House Historical Association

THE STAR-SPANGLED BANNER

Francis Scott Key

O say, can you see, by the dawn's early light,
What so proudly we hailed at the twilight's last gleaming—
Whose broad stripes and bright stars, through the perilous fight,
O'er the ramparts we watched were so gallantly streaming!
And the rocket's red glare, the bombs bursting in air,
Gave proof through the night that our flag was still there;
O say does that star-spangled banner yet wave
O'er the land of the free, and the home of the brave?

On that shore dimly seen through the mists of the deep,
Where the foe's haughty host in dread silence reposes,
What is that which the breeze, o'er the towering steep,
As it fitfully blows, now conceals, now discloses?
Now it catches the gleam of the morning's first beam,
In full glory reflected now shines on the stream;
'Tis the star-spangled banner; O long may it wave
O'er the land of the free, and the home of the brave!

And where is that band who so vauntingly swore
That the havoc of war and the battle's confusion
A home and a country should leave us no more?
Their blood has washed out their foul footstep's pollution.
No refuge could save the hireling and slave
From the terror of flight, or the gloom of the grave;
And the star-spangled banner in triumph doth wave
O'er the land of the free, and the home of the brave.

O thus be it forever, when free men shall stand
Between their loved homes and war's desolation!
Blest with victory and peace, may their heav'n rescued land
Praise the power that hath made and preserved us a nation.
Then conquer we must, when our cause it is just,
And this be our motto—"In God is our trust;"
And the star-spangled banner in triumph shall wave
O'er the land of the free, and the home of the brave.

An Inestimable Jewel

It is not merely for today but for all time to come that we should perpetuate for our children's children that great and free government which we have enjoyed all our lives. I beg you to remember this, not merely for my sake, but for yours. I happen, temporarily, to occupy the White House. I am a living witness that any one of your children may look to come here as my father's child has. It is in order that each one of you may have, through this free government which we have enjoyed, an open field and a fair chance for your industry, enterprise, and intelligence that you may all have equal privileges in the race of life, with all its desirable human aspirations. It is for this the struggle should be maintained that we may not lose our birthright—not only for one, but for two or three years. The nation is worth fighting for to secure such an inestimable jewel.

Abraham Lincoln

THE GETTYSBURG ADDRESS

Fourscore and seven years ago our fathers brought forth on this continent a new nation, conceived in liberty, and dedicated to the proposition that all men are created equal. Now we are engaged in a great civil war, testing whether that nation, or any nation so conceived and so dedicated, can long endure. We are met on a great battlefield of that war. We have come to dedicate a portion of that field as a final resting place for those who here gave their lives that that nation might live. It is altogether fitting and proper that we should do this. But, in a larger sense, we cannot dedicate—we cannot consecrate—we cannot hallow—this ground. The brave men, living and dead, who struggled here, have consecrated it far above our poor power to add or detract.

The world will little note nor long remember what we say here, but it can never forget what they did here. It is for us, the living, rather, to be dedicated here to the unfinished work which they who fought here have thus far so nobly advanced. It is rather for us to be here dedicated to the great task remaining before us—that from these honored dead we take increased devotion to that cause for which they gave the last full measure of devotion; that we here highly resolve that these dead shall not have died in vain; that this nation, under God, shall have a new birth of freedom; and that government of the people, by the people, for the people, shall not perish from the earth.

Abraham Lincoln

GATEWAY TO THE WEST

Man is capable of a limitless vision. The ability of our minds to imagine, together with the ability of our hands to build, allows man to dream his future and build that future according to his imagining.

A city like St. Louis can be thought of as a kind of culmination of the visions and dreams of many men. A city grows, as St. Louis did, from such meager dreams as the building of a log cabin on the west banks of the Mississippi River in 1764, where Pierre Laclede and Auguste Chouteau opened their fur-trading post.

On the banks of the Mississippi River at St. Louis, surrounded by a twentieth-century metropolis, we can look back at what came before us down the long river of geologic time, and we can look off toward the future and wonder which of man's imaginings will become reality in the year 2000 and beyond.

If future man comes upon this stainless-steel arch, the result of one man's imagining, he will have some notion of our dreams for the future. Stand under the Gateway Arch some full-moon night and listen as it reaches toward the stars and returns with their light. The arch is also a tribute to the dreams of our past: to the dreams of men like Thomas Jefferson, who negotiated the purchase of the Louisiana Territory; to the dreams of the explorers with Lewis and Clark, who headed west up the Missouri River in May 1804. After more than two years and 7,000 miles, they brought back word of the Pacific Ocean.

Measure the speed of jets across America today against the years since 1804. Man's imagination propels him quickly into the future.

Man has always been an explorer, adventuring out beyond the circle of fire, out beyond the flat maps of ancient cartographers marked with warnings that read "Here Be Monsters," out beyond the pull of earth's gravity. Man's future has first been man's dream of that future.

★★★★★ 30 ★★★★★

Photo Opposite
THE GATEWAY ARCH
St. Louis. Missouri
Gene Ahrens, Photographer

THE EMIGRANTS

John Greenleaf Whittier

We cross the prairie as of old
   The Pilgrims crossed the sea,
To make the West, as they the East,
   The homestead of the free.

We go to rear a wall of men
   On Freedom's southern line,
And plant beside the cotton tree
   The rugged Northern pine!

We're flowing from our native hills
   As our free rivers flow:
The blessing of our Mother-land
   Is on us as we go.

We go to plant her common schools
   On distant prairie swells,

And give the Sabbaths of the wild
   The music of her bells.

Upbearing, like the Ark of old,
   The Bible in our van,
We go to test the truth of God
   Against the fraud of man.

No pause, nor rest, save where the streams
   That feed the Kansas run,
Save where our Pilgrim gonfalon
   Shall flout the setting sun!

We'll tread the prairie as of old
   Our fathers sailed the sea,
And make the West, as they the East,
   The homestead of the free!

Photo Opposite
THE GRAND CANYON
Arizona
Ed Cooper, Photographer

AMERICA THE BEAUTIFUL

Katherine Lee Bates

Samuel A. Ward

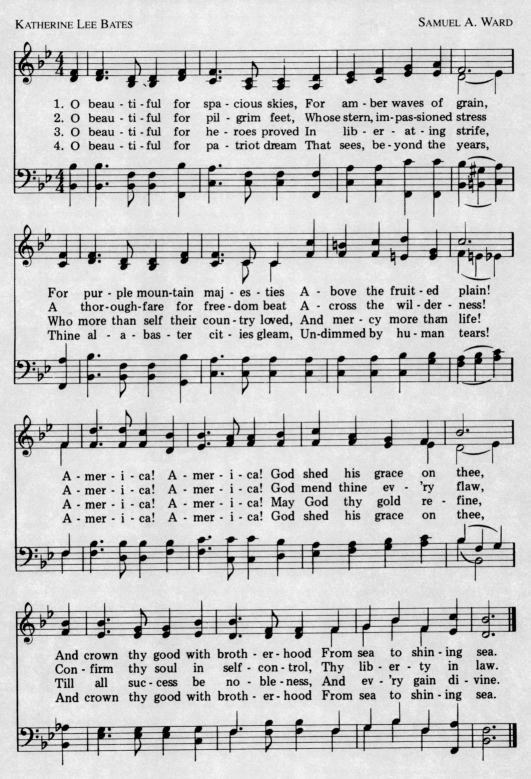

1. O beau - ti - ful for spa - cious skies, For am - ber waves of grain,
2. O beau - ti - ful for pil - grim feet, Whose stern, im - pas - sioned stress
3. O beau - ti - ful for he - roes proved In lib - er - at - ing strife,
4. O beau - ti - ful for pa - triot dream That sees, be - yond the years,

For pur - ple moun-tain maj - es - ties A - bove the fruit - ed plain!
A thor-ough-fare for free-dom beat A - cross the wil - der - ness!
Who more than self their coun - try loved, And mer - cy more than life!
Thine al - a - bas - ter cit - ies gleam, Un-dimmed by hu - man tears!

A - mer - i - ca! A - mer - i - ca! God shed his grace on thee,
A - mer - i - ca! A - mer - i - ca! God mend thine ev - 'ry flaw,
A - mer - i - ca! A - mer - i - ca! May God thy gold re - fine,
A - mer - i - ca! A - mer - i - ca! God shed his grace on thee,

And crown thy good with broth - er - hood From sea to shin - ing sea.
Con - firm thy soul in self - con - trol, Thy lib - er - ty in law.
Till all suc - cess be no - ble - ness, And ev - 'ry gain di - vine.
And crown thy good with broth - er - hood From sea to shin - ing sea.

THE NEW COLOSSUS

Emma Lazarus

Not like the brazen giant of Greek fame,
With conquering limbs astride from land to land;
Here at our sea-washed sunset gates shall stand
A mighty woman with a torch, whose flame
Is the imprisoned lightning, and her name
Mother of Exiles. From her beacon-hand
Glows world-wide welcome; her mild eyes command
The air-bridged harbor that twin-cities frame.
"Keep, ancient lands, your storied pomp!" cries she
With silent lips. "Give me your tired, your poor,
Your huddled masses yearning to breathe free,
The wretched refuse of your teeming shore.
Send these, the homeless, tempest-tossed to me—
I lift my lamp beside the golden door!"

How to Display the Flag

1. When the flag is suspended over a sidewalk, it should be hoisted out, union first, from the building.

2. The flag of the United States, when displayed with another flag against a wall from crossed staffs, should be on the flag's own right, and its staff should be in front of the staff of the other flag.

3. The flag, when flown at half staff, should be first hoisted to the peak for an instant and then lowered to half-staff position. The flag should be again raised to the peak before it is lowered for the day.

4. When flags of states, cities, or localities, or pennants of societies, are flown on the same halyard with the flag of the United States, the latter should always be at the peak. When the flags are flown from adjacent staffs, the flag of the United States should be hoisted first and lowered last. No such flag or pennant may be placed above or to the right of the flag of the United States.

5. When the flag is displayed over the middle of the street, it should be suspended vertically with the union to the north in an east and west street or to the east in a north and south street.

6. When the flag is displayed from a staff projecting horizontally or at an angle from the windowsill, balcony, or front of a building, the union should be placed at the peak of the staff unless the flag is at half staff.

7. When the flag is used to cover a casket, it should be so placed that the union is at the head and over the left shoulder. The flag should not be lowered into the grave or allowed to touch the ground.

8. When the flag is displayed in a manner other than by being flown from a staff, it should be displayed flat, indoors or out. When displayed either horizontally or vertically against a wall, the union should be uppermost and to the flag's own right. When displayed in a window it should be displayed in the same way, with the union to the left of the observer in the street. When festoons, rosettes, or drapings are desired, bunting of blue, white, and red should be used, but never the flag.

9. The flag, when carried in a procession with another flag or flags, should be either on the marching right—the flag's own right—or, if there is a line of other flags, in front of the center of that line.

10. The flag of the United States should be at the center and highest point of the group when a number of flags of states or localities or pennants of societies are grouped and displayed from staffs.

11. When flags of two or more nations are displayed, they are to be flown from separate staffs of the same height. The flags should be of approximately equal size. International usage forbids the display of the flag of one nation above that of another nation in time of peace.

Painting Opposite
THE PLEDGE OF ALLEGIANCE
John Slobodnik

America's Welcome Home

Henry van Dyke

Oh, gallantly they fared forth in khaki and in blue,
America's crusading host of warriors bold and true;
They battled for the rights of men beside our brave Allies.
And now they're coming home to us with glory in their eyes.

Oh it's home again, America for me!
Our hearts are turning home again and there we long to be,
In our beautiful big country beyond the ocean bars,
Where the air is full of sunlight and the flag is full of stars.

They bore our country's great word across the rolling sea,
"America swears brotherhood with all the just and free."
They wrote that word victorious on fields of mortal strife,
And many a valiant lad was proud to seal it with his life.

Oh, welcome home in Heaven's peace, dear spirits of the dead!
And welcome home ye living sons America hath bred!
The lords of war are beaten down, your glorious task is done;
You fought to make the whole world free, and the victory is won.

Now it's home again, and home again, our hearts are turning west,
Of all the lands beneath the sun America is best.
We're going home to our own folks, beyond the ocean bars,
Where the air is full of sunlight and the flag is full of stars.

THE GIFT OUTRIGHT

Robert Frost

The land was ours before we were the land's.
She was our land more than a hundred years
Before we were her people. She was ours
In Massachusetts, in Virginia,
But we were England's, still colonials,
Possessing what we still were unpossessed by,
Possessed by what we now no more possessed.
Something we were withholding made us weak
Until we found out that it was ourselves
We were withholding from our land of living,
And forthwith found salvation in surrender.
Such as we were we gave ourselves outright
(The deed of gift was many deeds of war)
To the land vaguely realizing westward,
But still unstoried, artless, unenhanced,
Such as she was, such as she would become.

Photo Opposite
THE TOMB OF THE UNKNOWN SOLDIER
Washington, D. C.
Dietrich Stock Photos

THE FOUR FREEDOMS

In the future days, which we seek to make secure, we look forward to a world founded upon four essential human freedoms.

The first is freedom of speech and expression—everywhere in the world.

The second is freedom of every person to worship God in his own way—everywhere in the world.

The third is freedom from want, which, translated into world terms, means economic understandings which will secure to every nation a healthy peacetime life for its inhabitants—everywhere in the world.

The fourth is freedom from fear, which, translated into world terms, means a worldwide reduction of armaments to such a point and in such a thorough fashion that no nation will be in a position to commit an act of physical aggression against any neighbor—anywhere in the world.

That is no vision of a distant millennium. It is a definite basis for a kind of world attainable in our own time and generation. That kind of world is the very antithesis of the so-called new order of tyranny which the dictators seek to create with the crash of a bomb.

Franklin D. Roosevelt

Painting Opposite
FREEDOM FROM FEAR
Norman Rockwell
© 1943 by Curtis Publishing Company

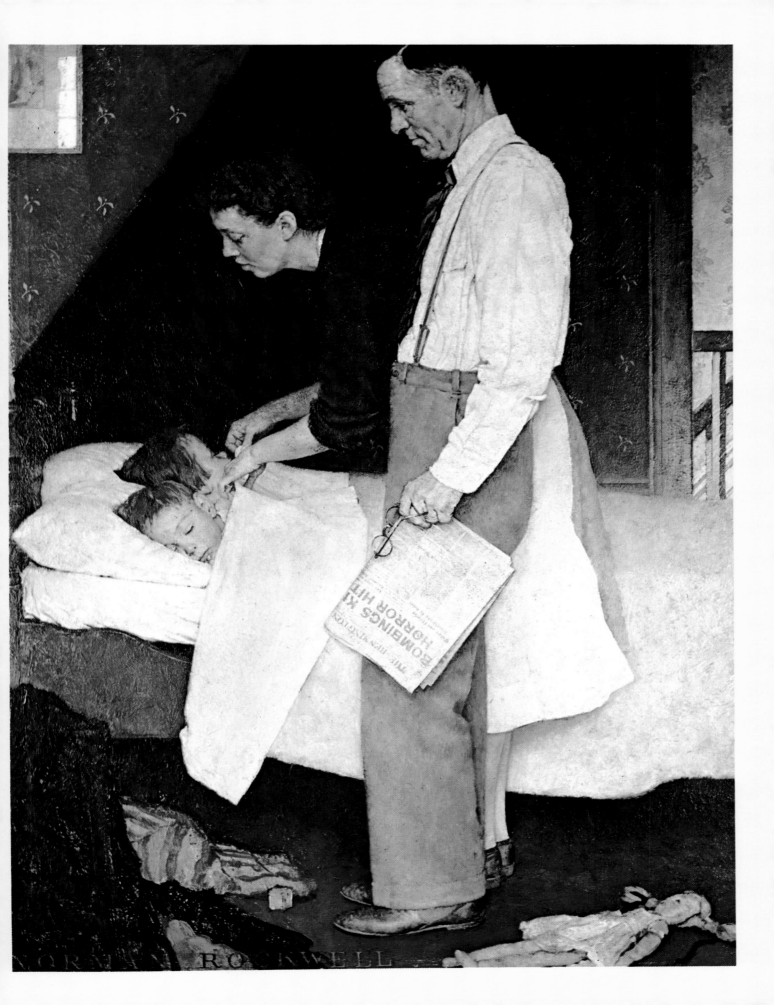

BOMBINGS KI...
HORROR HIT...

NORMAN ROCKWELL

FREEDOM OF WORSHIP

Grace Noll Crowell

Its eternal price is eternal vigilance,
And faith that sees the worth in any man;
The knowledge that no good thing comes by chance,
But must be labored for. Since time began
The struggle has been bitter, hard and long
To keep a principle intact and whole.
As mankind sought to shield from hurt and wrong
The priceless freedom of the human soul.

Hardships were there, and rough the frontiers crossed,
And blood was spilled upon embattled sod,
That men's religious freedom not be lost,
As conscientiously they worshiped God.
O men, keep faith! Fight ever valiantly
That this great basic freedom be kept free.

Painting Opposite
FREEDOM OF RELIGION
Norman Rockwell
© 1943 by Curtis Publishing Company

EACH ACCORDING TO THE DICTATES
OF HIS OWN CONSCIENCE

NORMAN ROCKWELL

ONE-THIRD A NATION

Here is the challenge to our democracy: in this nation I see tens of millions of its citizens—a substantial part of its whole population—who at this very moment are denied the greater part of what the very lowest standards of today call the necessities of life.

I see millions of families trying to live on incomes so meager that the pall of family disaster hangs over them day by day. I see millions whose daily lives in city and on farm continue under conditions labeled indecent by so-called polite society half a century ago. I see millions denied education, recreation, and the opportunity to better their lot and the lot of their children. I see millions lacking the means to buy the products of farmer and factory and by their poverty denying work and productiveness to other millions. I see one-third of a nation ill-housed, ill-clad, ill-nourished.

It is not in despair that I paint you that picture. I paint it for you in hope—because the nation, seeing and understanding the injustice in it, proposes to paint it out. We are determined to make every American citizen the subject of this country's interest and concern; and we will never regard any faithful, law-abiding group within our borders as superfluous. The test of our progress is not whether we add more to the abundance of those who have much; it is whether we provide enough for those who have too little.

Franklin D. Roosevelt

Painting Opposite
FREEDOM FROM WANT
Norman Rockwell
© 1943 by Curtis Publishing Company

FREEDOM OF SPEECH

The Americans of all nations at any time upon the earth have probably the fullest poetical nature. The United States themselves are essentially the greatest poem . . . Here is not merely a nation but a teeming nation of nations . . . Here is the hospitality which forever indicates heroes.

Other states indicate themselves in their deputies . . . but the genius of the United States is not best or most in its executives or legislatures, nor in its ambassadors or authors or colleges or churches or parlors, nor even in its newspapers and inventors . . . but always most in the common people. Their manners, speech, dress, friendships . . . their deathless attachment to freedom . . . the air they have of persons who never knew how it felt to stand in the presence of superiors . . . the fluency of their speech—these too are unrhymed poetry.

Walt Whitman

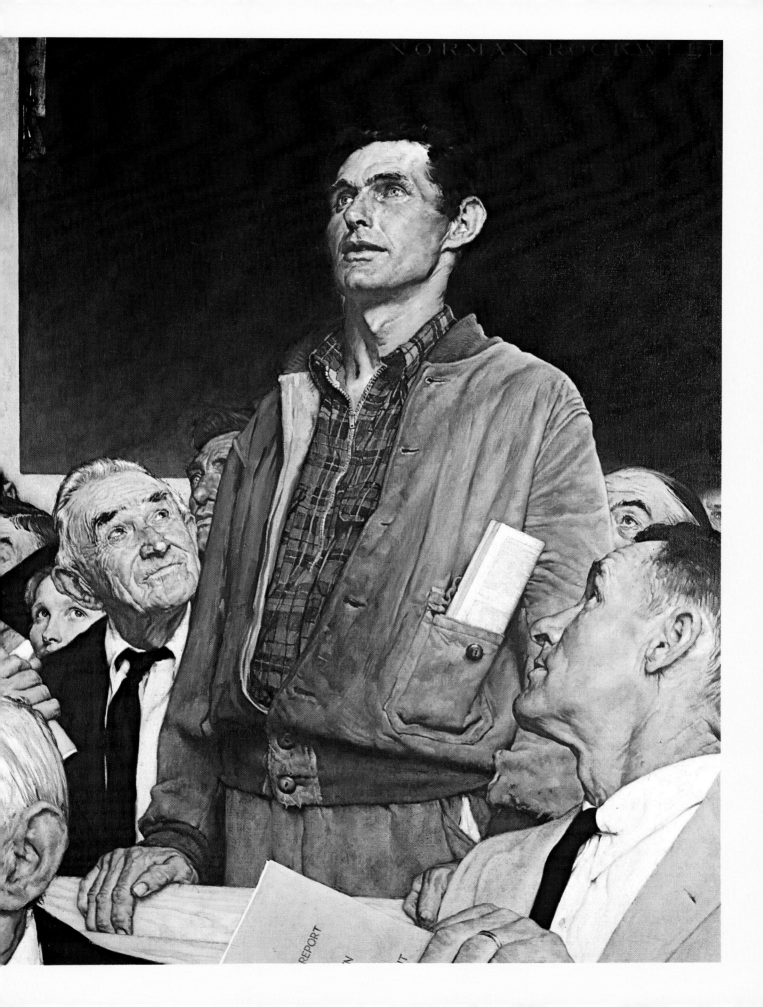

THE RIGHT
IS MORE PRECIOUS
THAN THE PEACE

It is a fearful thing to lead this great peaceful people into war . . . but the right is more precious than peace, and we shall fight for the things which we have always carried nearest our hearts—for democracy, for the right of those who submit to authority to have a voice in their own governments, for the rights and liberties of small nations, for a universal dominion of right by such a concert of free peoples as shall bring peace and safety to all nations and make the world itself at last free. To such a task we can dedicate our lives and our fortunes, everything that we are and everything that we have, with the pride of those who know that the day has come when America is privileged to spend her blood and her might for the principles that gave her birth and the peace which she has treasured. God helping her, she can do no other.

Woodrow Wilson

OXER·REBELLION·1900 ⁕ NICARAGUA·1912 ⁕ VERA·CRUZ·1914 ⁕ HAITI·1915-1934 ⁕ SANTO·DOMINGO·1916-1924 ⁕ WORLD·WAR·I·1917-1918 BELLEAU·WOO

IN·HONOR·AND·MEMORY
OF·THE·MEN·OF·THE
UNITED·STATES·MARINE·CORPS
WHO·HAVE·GIVEN
THEIR·LIVES·TO·THEIR·COUNTRY
SINCE·10·NOVEMBER·1775

A Symbol of Strength

Pamela Kennedy

The sun streaks the sky above the misty mountains with reds and oranges, and the doves and cardinals begin their early conversations. In the harbor, small boats and tugs commence their morning chores, hauling, pushing, and scurrying about the Navy's business. It is morning in Pearl Harbor, and outside my window I see the waterfront awaken. Soon the sounds of engines and ships, splashing wakes, and tooting whistles will drown out the birds, and the day's business will be underway.

But now, when things are still just shaking off the night's cool grasp, I walk across the dew-damp grass to stand behind the white curve of the USS *Arizona* Memorial and watch the sun come up.

We live on tiny Ford Island in the middle of the harbor and have a private view of this most public spectacle. It is a monument I have come to love, not only for what it brings to mind of past events, but for what it says to me of America now and in the future.

The slender, white saddle of concrete sits astride a sunken battleship, its twenty-one open windows a silent salute to the fallen ones whose names are engraved upon its marble walls. Each day thousands of visitors take the five-minute boat ride out to stroll the breezy corridor and gaze into the water below. They come to try and understand something of what our country was and what it is meant to be.

The monument, built upon the wreckage of a war, reflects simplicity and strength, confirming to all who visit that America is a land where men can triumph over wrong. Spanning the sunken *Arizona*'s hull, the monument is a bridge from past to present, from despair to hope. It is this aspect of the shrine which draws me most, for I am an optimist. I see America's hopes and dreams still bright in her people.

It is easy to cast a cynical eye upon our nation, to complain about her weaknesses and wail about her woes. That's why I come here in the morning light to see in simple lines and clear cut angles a symbol of her strength. At 8:00 A.M. the bugle sounds and the flag is raised. *The Star Spangled Banner* drifts across the harbor; my heart swells with pride. Here, in the midst of the world's greatest ocean, the words seem true. America is still the land of the free and, with God's help, will continue to be the home of the brave.

USS *ARIZONA* MEMORIAL
Pearl Harbor
Oahu, Hawaii
H. Armstrong Roberts

THE TORCH IS PASSED

Man holds in his mortal hands the power to abolish all forms of human poverty and all forms of human life. And yet the same revolutionary beliefs for which our forebearers fought are still at issue around the globe—the belief that the rights of man come not from the generosity of the state but from the hand of God.

We dare not forget today that we are the heirs of that first revolution. Let the word go forth from this time and place, to friend and foe alike, that the torch has been passed to a new generation of Americans—born in this century, tempered by war, disciplined by a hard and bitter peace, proud of our ancient heritage—and unwilling to witness or permit the slow undoing of those human rights to which this nation has always been committed, and to which we are committed today at home and around the world.

Let every nation know, whether it wishes us well or ill, that we shall pay any price, bear any burden, meet any hardship, support any friend, oppose any foe to assure the survival and the success of liberty. . . .

In the long history of the world, only a few generations have been granted the role of defending freedom in its hour of maximum danger. I do not shrink from this responsibility—I welcome it. I do not believe that any of us would exchange places with any other people or any other generation. The energy, the faith, the devotion which we bring to this endeavor will light our country and all who serve it—and the glow from that fire can truly light the world.

And so, my fellow Americans: ask not what your country can do for you—ask what you can do for your country.

My fellow citizens of the world: ask not what America will do for you, but what together we can do for the freedom of man.

Finally, whether you are citizens of America or citizens of the world, ask of us here the same high standards of strength and sacrifice which we ask of you. With a good conscience our only sure reward, with history the final judge of our deeds, let us go forth to lead the land we love, asking His blessing and His help, but knowing that here on earth God's work must truly be our own.

John F. Kennedy

Photo Opposite
AIR FORCE ACADEMY CHAPEL
Colorado Springs, Colorado
Richard Carkeek, Cyr Color Photo
Agency

REFLECTIONS AFTER RETURNING FROM THE MOON

We landed on the Sea of Tranquility, in the cool of the early lunar morning, when the long shadows would aid our perception.

The sun was only ten degrees above the horizon, while the earth turned through nearly a full day during our stay, the sun at Tranquility Base rose barely eleven degrees . . . a small fraction of the month-long lunar day. There was a peculiar sensation of the duality of time . . . the swift rush of events that characterizes all our lives . . . and the ponderous parade which makes the aging of the universe. . . .

In the next twenty centuries, the age of Aquarius of the great year, the age for which our young people have such high hopes, humanity may begin to understand its most baffling mystery . . . where are we going? The earth is, in fact, traveling many thousands of miles per hour in the direction of the constellation Hercules . . . to some unknown destination in the cosmos. Man must understand his universe in order to understand his destiny.

Mystery creates wonder and wonder is the basis for man's desire to understand. Who knows what mysteries will be solved in our lifetime, and what new riddles will become the challenge of the new generations? Science has not mastered prophecy. We predict too much for the next year and yet far too little for the next ten. Responding to challenge is one of democracy's great strengths. Our success in space leads us to hope that this strength can be used in the next decade in the solution of many of our planet's problems.

Neil A. Armstrong

Photo Opposite
MOON LANDING

The noise of passing feet
On the prairie . . .
Is it men or gods
Who come out of the silence?

Chippewa Indian Saying

GREAT MEN

Lord Byron

Tis the spirit
   of the single mind
Makes that of multitudes
   take one direction,
As roll the waters
   to the breathing wind,
Or roams the herd beneath
   the bull's protection;

Or as a little dog
   will lead the blind,
Or a bell-wether form
   the flock's connection
By tinkling sounds,
   when they go forth to victual;—
Such is the way
   of great men o'er little.

★★★★★ **60** ★★★★★

Photo Opposite
APOLLO 14 LAUNCH
Cape Kennedy, Florida
Bill Lees, Cyr Color Photo Agency

LET'S BE BRAVE

Edgar A. Guest

Let's be brave when the laughter dies
And the tears come into our troubled eyes,
Let's cling to the faith and the old belief
When the skies grow gray with the clouds of grief,
Let's bear the sorrow and hurt and pain
And wait till the laughter comes again.

Let's be brave when the trials come
And our hearts are sad and our lips are dumb,
Let's strengthen ourselves in the times of test
By whispering softly that God knows best;
Let us still believe, though we cannot know,
We shall learn sometime it is better so.

Let's be brave when the joy departs,
Till peace shall come to our troubled hearts,
For the tears must fall and the rain come down
And each brow be pressed to the thorny crown;
Yet after dark shall the sun arise,
So let's be brave when the laughter dies.

EQUALITY

I speak tonight for the dignity of man and the destiny of democracy. I urge every member of both parties, Americans of all religions and of all colors, from every section of the country, to join me in that cause . . . for the cries of pain and the hymns of protest of oppressed people have summoned into convocation all the majesty of this great government of the greatest nation on earth.

Our mission is at once the oldest and the most basic of this country: to right wrong, to do justice, to serve man.

In our time we have come to live with moments of great crisis. Our lives have been marked by debate about great issues, issues of war and peace, issues of prosperity and depression. But rarely in any time does an issue lay bare the secret heart of America itself. Rarely are we met with a challenge, not to our growth or abundance, or our welfare or security, but rather to the values and the purpose and the meaning of our beloved nation.

The issue of equal rights . . . is such an issue. And should we defeat every enemy, and should we double our wealth, and conquer the stars, and still be unequal to this issue, then we will have failed as a people and as a nation.

The time of justice has now come. I tell you that I believe sincerely that no force can hold it back. It is right in the eyes of man and God that it should come. And when it does, I think that day will brighten the life of every American.

Lyndon B. Johnson

THE SAME VOICE SOUNDS

A POEM FOR THE 4TH OF JULY

Margaret Rorke

When we celebrate the birthday of America this year,
Names of people first and famous are the ones we're sure to hear,
But we mustn't for a moment miss the many all unsung
Who in quiet did their duty and in virtue raised their young.

All unheralded they've labored in the factories and fields.
They have made their nation's armies; they have gathered in the yields.
From her veins, her seas, and rivers, they have given heart and mind
To discover her best secrets and to keep her name enshrined.

When our legacy is valued, when our growth is duly weighed,
We must look beneath the surface where the leaders are portrayed
For the millions who've supported with their lives and minds and might
What they've loved and truly trusted as the flesh and blood of right.

AMERICA

Samuel Francis Smith

My country, 'tis of thee,
Sweet land of liberty,
   Of thee I sing;
Land where my fathers died,
Land of the pilgrims' pride.
From every mountainside
   Let freedom ring.

My native country, thee,
Land of the noble free,—
   Thy name I love;
I love thy rocks and rills,
Thy woods and templed hills:
My heart with rapture thrills
   Like that above.

Let music swell the breeze,
And ring from all the trees,
   Sweet Freedom's song;
Let mortal tongues awake,
Let all that breathe partake,
Let rocks their silence break,—
   The sound prolong.

Our fathers' God, to Thee,
Author of liberty,
   To thee we sing;
Long may our land be bright
With Freedom's holy light;
Protect us by Thy might,
   Great God, our King.

AMONG DAKOTA'S HILLS

Frank Manhart

No crumbling stone—no mellow rock
The sculptor seeks where to reveal
The foremost men of hardy stock
Who served their country with rare zeal.

Among Dakota's hills so grand
The storms of time that never cease
Touch lightly mighty crags that stand
Where Borglum carves his masterpiece!

What if stone is a toilsome page?
How could a truly mindful son
Forget in this the golden age
The blessings the brave fathers won?

Look up, all you patriots true!
Where once the bare rock outward spread,
There valiant men have come in view.
Their deeds still live—they are not dead.

Our Washington warns of foreign foe,
Who would assail our shores again;
While Jefferson would have us know
That tyrants rise 'mongst thoughtless men.

Our Lincoln pleads for greater faith
In boundless power of the right
To hold intact the Ship of State,
And overcome opposing might.

There's Roosevelt who could inspire
His fellow man to seek high goals,
And hold to a wholesome desire,
And not to plead for grants and doles.

O Carver of the Noble Brow,
Hath ever other dreamer known
Such inspiration as yours now
To carve life into lifeless stone?

THE SPIRIT OF LIBERTY

We have gathered here to affirm a faith, a faith in a common purpose, a common conviction, a common devotion. Some of us have chosen America as the land of our adoption; the rest have come from those who did the same. For this reason we have some right to consider ourselves a picked group, a group of those who had the courage to break from the past and brave the dangers and loneliness of a strange land.

What was the object that nerved us, or those who went before us, to this choice? We sought liberty; freedom from oppression, freedom from want, freedom to be ourselves. This we then sought. This we now believe that we are by way of winning.

What do we mean when we say that first of all we seek liberty? I often wonder whether we do not rest our hopes too much upon constitutions, upon laws and upon courts. These are false hopes; believe me, these are false hopes. Liberty lies in the hearts of men and women. When it dies there, no constitution, no law, no court can save it. No constitution, no law, no court can even do much to help it. While it lies there, it needs no constitution, no law, no court to save it.

And what is this liberty that must lie in the hearts of men and women? It is not the ruthless, the unbridled will. It is not freedom to do as one likes. That is the denial of liberty, and leads straight to its overthrow. A society in which men recognize no check upon their freedom soon becomes a society where freedom is the possession of only a savage few; as we have learned to our sorrow.

What then is the spirit of liberty? I cannot define it; I can only tell you my own faith. The spirit of liberty is the spirit which is not too sure that it is right. The spirit of liberty is the spirit which seeks to understand the minds of other men and women. The spirit of liberty is the spirit which weighs their interests alongside its own without bias. The spirit of liberty remembers that not even a sparrow falls to earth unheeded. The spirit of liberty is the spirit of Him who, near two thousand years ago, taught mankind that lesson it has never learned, but has never quite forgotten: that there may be a kingdom where the least shall be heard and considered side by side with the greatest.

And now in that spirit, that spirit of an America which has never been, and which never may be; nay, which never will be, except as the conscience and courage of Americans create it; yet in the spirit of that America that lies hidden in some form in the aspirations of us all; in the spirit of that America for which our young are at this moment fighting and dying; in that spirit of liberty and of America I ask you to rise with me and to pledge our faith in the glorious destiny of our beloved country—with liberty and justice for all.

Learned Hand

BE STRONG

Maltbie D. Babcock

Be strong!
We are not here to play,—to dream, to drift.
We have hard work to do and loads to lift.
Shun not the struggle,—face it: 'tis God's gift.

Be strong!
Say not the days are evil. Who's to blame?
And fold the hands and acquiesce,—O shame!
Stand up, speak out, and bravely, in God's name.

Be strong!
It matters not how deep entrenched the wrong,
How hard the battle goes, the day how long;
Faint not,—fight on! Tomorrow comes the song.

I HEAR AMERICA SINGING

Walt Whitman

I hear America singing, the varied carols I hear,
Those of mechanics, each one singing his as it should be
    blithe and strong,
The carpenter singing his as he measures plank and beam,
The mason singing his as he makes ready for work,
    or leaves off work,
The boatman singing what belongs to him on his boat,
    the deckhand singing on the steamboat deck,
The shoemaker singing as he sits on his bench,
    the hatter singing as he stands.
The wood-cutter's song, the ploughboy's on his way
    in the morning, or at noon intermission or at sundown,
The delicious singing of the mother, or of the young wife at work,
    or of the girl sewing and washing,
Each singing what belongs to him or her and to none else,
The day what belongs to the day—at night the party
    of young fellows, robust, friendly,
Singing with open mouths their strong melodious songs.

Photo Opposite
AMERICAN CHILDREN
Robert Hayes, Photographer

THE HEART OF AMERICA

Whatever America hopes
To bring to pass in the world
Must first come to pass
In the heart of America.
The peace we seek, then,
Is nothing less than
The practice and fulfillment
Of our whole faith,
Among ourselves
And in our dealings with others.

This signifies more
Than the stilling of guns,
Easing the sorrow of war.
More than escape from death,
It is a way of life.
More than a haven for the weary,
It is a hope for the brave.

This is the hope
That beckons us onward . . .
This is the work that awaits us all,
To be done with bravery, with charity,
And with prayer to Almighty God.

Dwight D. Eisenhower

INDEX

ACKNOWLEDGMENTS

REFLECTIONS AFTER RETURNING FROM THE MOON by Neil A. Armstrong: Used by permission of the author. AMERICA THE BEAUTIFUL reprinted from the 1975 BAPTIST HYMNAL: Used by permission of the Baptist Sunday School Board/Broadman Press. FREEDOM OF WORSHIP from APPLES OF GOLD by Grace Noll Crowell. Copyright © 1950 by Harper & Brothers, Inc. Reprinted by permission of HarperCollins Publishers. THE GIFT OUTRIGHT from THE POETRY OF ROBERT FROST, edited by Edward Connery Latham. Copyright 1942 by Robert Frost. Copyright © 1969 by Holt, Rinehart, and Winston. Copyright © 1970 by Leslie Frost Ballantine. Reprinted by permission of Henry Holt and Company, Inc. LET'S BE BRAVE by Edgar A. Guest: Used by permission of the estate. GATEWAY TO THE WEST reprinted from MISSOURI; FACES AND PLACES by Wes Lyle and John Hall. Copyright © 1977 by Regents Press of Kansas (now University Press of Kansas). AMONG DAKOTA'S HILLS from THE CLAN AND OTHER POEMS. Copyright © 1953 by Frank Manhart: Used by permission of the estate. AMERICA'S WELCOME HOME by Henry van Dyke from THE POEMS OF HENRY VAN DYKE: Reprinted by permission of Charles Scribner's Sons, an imprint of MacMillan Publishing Company. Copyright © 1918, 1919 by Charles Scribner's Sons. Copyrights renewed.

Front Cover
AMERICAN FLAG
H. Armstrong Roberts

Back Cover
THE CAPITOL AT NIGHT
Jack Zehrt, Photographer